Looking Good, Mary

Mary Robinson

Clink Street

Published by Clink Street Publishing 2022

Copyright © 2022

First edition.

ISBNs:
978-1-914498-70-1 – paperback
978-1-914498-71-8 – ebook

To my darling daughter, I have you to thank for this.

Introduction

Life is so different, particularly for a woman in your 40s when you have to start all over again as I have, and without a man. This book is about everyday events that have personally happened to me.

Names have been changed to protect those in question, though I have used my ex- husband's name as I know that he wouldn't mind and would probably laugh to know that he is in my book. Unfortunately, he is no longer with us after taking his life in 2008. I do sometimes wonder "Why me?", does this happen to other people? Of course it does, but nothing makes it easier when it's happening to you.

I am seriously blonde, and have been told that I am a rare breed! I don't think so I'm just me and as I seem to have had a pretty colourful life, I thought I would share some of my past and present with you. I've put the bad behind me, and look forward to the future. "Think positive" my dad used to say, and I do.

So, with my daughter now living with me, I move on. We were lying in bed one night talking between rooms and I was saying how I wished I was rich and what I would do if I was. It was then that she said, "Hey Mum why don't you write, you are so good at it?", and it all started when we went to Vegas just after Chris had died.

I kept a diary, which is how the book began.

And when I was rock bottom, I felt it and taught my parrot to say "Looking good Mary" which, yes she did say – and still does. So no matter how bad I felt, she always cheered me up. That is why I chose to call my book *Looking Good, Mary*.

The Beginning

We are now in a credit crunch the telly says it all,
With growing unemployment, and prices that will fall.
But every day it worries me, it's like a massive stitch
I'm fed up being poor – if only I were rich.
I lay in bed at night and think – what is there I can do,
That'll bring me in some money, and stop me feeling blue?
I am a Norland Nanny, and children I do love,
But recently my life has changed – is there a God above?
So with pen poised and fire lit I slowly start to write,
Of things that happen every day,
that give me strength to fight.
So I'm hoping that you'll read my poems,
and treat them like an itch,
That constantly need scratching
and they'll one day make me rich.

***

Starting Boarding School

I consider myself so incredibly lucky to have had
the childhood that I had,
With a Mum and Dad and two sisters,
though a brother wouldn't have been bad.
The time had come and a decision was made,
that we should go away,
To a boarding school in Ditchingham,
this wasn't too far away.
At the time it all seemed daunting,
and a really massive move,
But looking back I realise now
how prudish it would prove.
All my clothes were neatly labelled with
MARY NEEDS in black,
And each one had to be stitched by hand,
right down to the outdoor mack.
It was All Hallows School for girls,
which was a convent that had nuns,
And to me at the age of twelve,
that didn't sound much fun.
My trunk was packed with uniform,
mufti shoes and socks,
And stood beside was a smallish trunk,
which was known as my 'Tuck Box'.

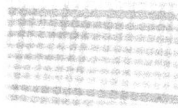

It was crammed right full with chocolate biscuits,
sweets and sherbet drops,
And crunchy things when put in mouth
would crackle snap and pop.
We had to be at school by noon,
as it was frowned upon if late,
So Mum stuck her foot down pronto,
and briskly reached the gates,
Where the sign read All Hallows School for Girls,
then my stomach really churned,
Was I really going away to leave my parents
for whom I'd yearn?
A sixth form girl she greeted us
"Do you want to come with me?"
And she led us up and up the stairs,
to a little dormitory.
The beds were scattered round the room
and I finally dropped my trunk,

Beside a massive skyscraper,
I was on the bottom bunk!
That took some getting used to,
getting jiggled like a stick,
Every time the other moved
it made you feel quite sick.

At 7.20 in the morning sharp,
the bell would ring on time,
To get us up, washed and dressed
and downstairs to form a line.
Breakfast always smelled so good
and nobody was ever late,
To miss the sausage eggs and bacon
that was put upon our plates.
The food it was delicious,
and matron always made sure,
That nobody left the table hungry,
and could always ask for more.
7.30pm lights-out time,
Matron ordered us all in bed,

I negotiated the metal bar so as not to bang my head.
"Lights out now," she said,
"there mustn't be any talking."
Surely that's impossible
for youngsters who are always squawking.
As it was a convent school,
the chapel was a must,
And it seemed that we were constantly there,
from morning, noon till dusk.
But my love of music took a grip,
and soon it would aspire,
And I joined the team with Sister Sheila
that formed the convent choir.
I simply just adored it and never made a fuss,
And yes, we probably were there it seemed
from morning, noon till dusk.
We would hammer out those songs,
and sing our hearts aloud,
And I'm sure that even God above
would think we'd done him proud.
Always on a Thursday night,
after practice we would flee
Like rockets back to main school
to see the highlights on TV,
Which was in those days *Top of the Pops*
which seemed tremendous fun,
And if you legged it quick enough,
you'd catch the Number One!

Getting confirmed was a major thing
when you went to a convent school,
Preparation was essential,
so on the day you didn't look a fool.
I had a brand-new dress,
common prayer book and bright white socks,
But panic set in on close examination –
I'd caught the chicken pox.
"It's no good ducky," said Matron
"You'll have to stay in bed."
And the rest of the girls were lucky
as the service went ahead.
So guess what happened,
because I was sick and on the pillow my head laid,
I was confirmed in the little school chapel,
and history I had made.

Saint Gabriel's was a dormitory
that was furthest from the Head,

So you could get away with mischief
when you should be tucked up in bed.
The shiny floor was perfect
and with just socks on your feet,
With opened doors you could skid right through
which was fun and pretty neat.
But as per usual it got out of hand
and somebody cracked their head,
And landed at the foot of matron who yelled,
"Get back into bed"!
The weeks were regimentally run and all rolled into one,
But weekends they were different,
and sometimes real good fun.
On Saturday afternoons, we'd sit around and talk
Till a sixth former would announce,
"C'mon we're going for a walk".
So with boots, hats and coats put on we formed a crocodile
And they frogmarched us round the countryside,
which seemed for endless miles.
Our legs would ache, our faces red
and boy did some of us moan,
"Are we ever going to turn around
and make our way back home?"
And home is what we called it,
and I know it sounds insane,
But if I had the chance to relive my life
I'd do it all again.
I sometime dream of my days at school,

for such happy days they were,
And it gave me the confidence and stability
that I have today for sure.
As I slowly progressed to sixth form,
I was in the lucky class
That a sixth form house would be built for us,
and the plans had just been passed.
We slowly watched it grow,
and it was tempting not to peep,
As furniture was assembled,
and built-in rooms where we'd sleep.
A spiral staircase was fitted, and ages it did take,
Unlucky for the person in the room next door,
cos the room walls they did shake!
I had my final year there, and reaped the benefits,
And for my leaving party – I ordered loads of chips
From the local fish and chip shop, which really wasn't far,
And I was one of the lucky ones who owned a little car.
The whole form was invited, the Head and Matron too,
The people in the chip shop laughed
when the order it came through.
"Hello," I said, "it's me – I was wondering if you could do
A massive order of chips with vinegar in bags for 42?"
It must have looked a funny sight,
us all sat on the floor,
Plonked on bean bags randomly,
that spread beyond the door.

The end of term service had come,
and no matter how I tried,
That dreaded song Jerusalem –
I sobbed and choked and cried,
And looking back I realise now,
my parents I thank them for
Sending me to such a wonderful school,
that doesn't exist anymore.

***

Norlands

I am a Norland Nanny,
You know the ones you see,
Pushing great big prams in uniform,
Hat, gloves, brown coat – that's me.
The college then was set in Berkshire
in truly beautiful grounds,
Where eventually along a massive drive set back,
the house did stand.
It looked just like a stately home
with a huge big entrance door,
And great big pillars and windows too
that reached from sky to floor.
But this wasn't where I was to sleep, no;
I was to follow the clock
That led me down a drive, round the corner
to a building called Stable Block.

I shared a room with three other girls
and it is only fair to say,
That we formed a friendship that has never died,
and I keep in touch today.
The course was quite intensive,
with lectures and lots to do,
From making wooden toys, rag dolls,
wall hangings to name a few.
But for me the nightmare started
when I had to learn to knit,
A garment for a baby or a toddler that would fit.
The pattern looked a simple one of a tiny baby's dress,
And I got as far as the ornate bit –
my god it looked a mess!
I couldn't work out how to pick up, drop or where it went,
And the more I knitted the worse it got
and was resembling a tent.
So then I thought, "I've cracked it,"
and zoomed ahead with pride,
Until I noticed Pat was standing closely by my side.
"Mary sweetie, can I look and see just what's gone wrong?
The back it should be three and its now ten inches long!"
This blasted dress I know I'll never get to hand it in,
I've redone the back five times and it's doing my head in.
But good ol' Pat she must've thought
"Oh poor old Mary she
Will never get to do this right – oh give it here to me."
And yes, she did complete it,

And breezed it with a song
And the back did measure three
Instead of ten inches long.
Throughout the course you have to care
for babies age 0–10,
And on this particular morning
I was presented with baby Ben.
His mother dropped him off at nine
and I was to have him for the day,
And at three months old a bonny boy,
we'd gurgle sit and play.
But as a senior nurse,
it was my job to show the students how
To bath a baby, top and tail – you know.
So round the bed they sat and the baby I held tight,
And told them all to please be quiet
so as not to scare the little mite.
There seemed an awful lot of them
all crammed around the door,
As I gently lowered the baby,
the bath collapsed on the floor.
The water just shot everywhere it was a sight to see,
And baby Ben oblivious just cooed and caahed at me.
All was fine where we were concerned
but below in baby day care,
Singing songs in a circle, water dripped everywhere.
I caused an utter panic and it was clearly plain to see
That water dripping everywhere was simply down to me.

I tried to keep composed and not to give up and run,
But the students thought the whole thing
was simply tremendous fun.
"In future," said young Rosie, "when we need to see a bath,
We'll request that it is Mary, cos at least you get a laugh!"
My six-week child was Thomas,
a Down's Syndrome boy of three,
Who I absolutely adored and I'm sure he did of me.
Funnily enough the weekends
were similar to being at school,
Though the difference being now
it was us that set the rules.
So down town we would trundle
our children in pushchairs,
We would always cause a stir as people
looked and talked and stared.
Depending on how good they were
we'd stop at shop for a treat,
And buy them all a lollipop
which Thomas thought was neat.
But on this particular occasion
he came in the shop with me,
He very nicely held my hand and little did I see.
The long old walk back home
really did make our legs ache,
But if we hurried back quick enough,
we'd be in time for chocolate cake.
We rushed into the refectory just to catch a cup of tea,

It was only then a casting eye of Thomas did I see.
His trouser pockets were crammed with sweets,
no wonder he didn't talk,
He was concentrating far too hard
to hide them as he walked.
I can't believe he'd grabbed them
quickly while I'd stopped,
So back we walked a pretty pace
to return them to the shop.
It was during my time at college
that I met a man called Chris,
Who undoubtedly captured my heart
though at the time I repeatedly dismissed.
I completed all my course work and all my lectures too,
In between looking after babies of which there were a few.
Twice a week in mornings I'd catch the bus at eight,
That would take me quite a distance
to a school with wrought-iron gates.
It was these next few weeks that really taught me
what life was all about,
As these deprived children expressed their anger,
and would fight and scream and shout.
They mostly came from families that somehow didn't care,
That their children smelt of urine
and they never washed their hair.
But this didn't faze me, I loved each and every one,
And grew so very close to them
that David called me Mum.

The mornings always started with songs
where we would clap,
And inevitably there was always one
that would end up on my lap.
It seemed that all was needed was a little love and care,
Life for some of these little ones seemed incredibly unfair.
Needless to say the time had come for me to now depart,
These somewhat neglected children
had left an imprint on my heart.
I wonder what the future holds for Abbey, Sam and Ben,
I can only hope the love I gave
will remain with each of them.
Our time at college had flown past
bringing it all to a close,
We had to have our work completed
which kept us on our toes.
The garden party was quite a thing and open house for all
To come and see our college work
that hung around the walls.
After college was hospital, a three-month stint for me,
And three other girls I joined in a flat in Salisbury.
It was a really fun time of working on delivery ward,
The shifts were long so playing was out
and we all could ill afford.
Helping mums with newborn babies
really put us to the test,
And trying to convince the bottle-fed ones
that breast is always best.

Another part of training that they encourage us all to do
Is working on the geriatric ward –
not for me I can tell you.
Don't get me wrong I love old people
even if they do all seem to shout,
But when it came to bed bathing –
blancmangie bits are out!
It was that that made me realise, no matter what they say
I couldn't work with the elderly – its babies all the way.
My three-week stint on geriatric ward
was quickly terminated
I simply couldn't do it and all the staff just got frustrated!

***

This next poem happened when I was working in Windsor
for my nine months' probation just after I had left college.

The Snake

A friend of mine worked down the road,
At a vets which wasn't far,
And sometimes in the evenings
I'd go and see her in my car.
We were chatting having coffee,
When a knock came at the door,
And there stood a frantic woman,
With a snake that touched the floor.
"You have to help me darling,
It's my Oscar, he's not well."
This massive snake around her neck,
Was more than sick I could tell.
We took her in the back room,
Where she gently laid him down,

I looked at Steff alarmingly
And our faces began to frown.
This lady hadn't noticed,
And it simply had to be said,
That Oscar's performing days were over;
He was well and truly dead.
The lady was beside herself,
And couldn't stop the tears,
As Oscar had been her livelihood,
He'd performed with her for years.
We made her a cup of coffee,
And she sat and had a moan
Till eventually she left with Oscar,
To bury him at her home.

My First Job

My first job took me to Windsor
with a little girl who was fine,
Mother worked in cabin crew which meant
Dad was about all the time.
At three years old and with one to one
she'd have a lot to say,
And daily walks we'd take to town
and she'd chatter all the way.
We'd often walk to the castle,
which was only just round the bend,
And then slowly take 'The Long Walk'
to the bronze horse at the end.
It really was a marathon and to help the time pass,
I'd always pack a picnic and we'd sit down on the grass,
To feast ourselves on sandwiches
and crackers with bits of cheese,
Followed by prawn-flavoured crisps,
that warranted a "Please."
Sometimes if the timing was right
though it really was quite hard,
We'd run to catch the soldiers
and the changing of the guards.
At weekends I would have time off
as that time was for me,
And I'd go and meet up with Chris

who was still going out with me.
Again my time at Windsor had quickly come to an end,
I tooted the horn and waved goodbye
till round the final bend.
I worked for many families with their children I did care,
And went with them on holiday
which took me everywhere.
Another job I took in Newbury which at first I wasn't sure,
They had two children an Alsatian and a lovely Labrador –
Which gave birth to a litter of puppies,
that all did well except one,
That didn't make up like the others
and couldn't feed from mum.
It was obvious to see that this pup would die,
I couldn't let this happen, I'd give it my best and try.
So sitting on a hot water bottle,
wrapped in a blanket and all through the night,
I fed the puppy hourly to save the little mite –
And save I did, she thrived, though always sat alone,
And as the others were slowly sold,
I knew she'd find no home.
Apart from loving the family
and the children from the start,
I dreaded leaving the puppy
who had grown close to my heart.
The morning of me leaving
as I was brushing my golden locks,
The family came up to my room and handed me a box.

"We want to give this as a gift – she loves you most of all,
You saved her life right from the start
when she was very small."
My eyes welled up as I lifted the lid and looking in did see,
The little puppy sitting there gazing up at me.

"What are you going to call her Mary?
She'll bring you so much fun."
"Penny," was my answer, cos she didn't cost me one.
I did a bit of temping then
which was short furious and fast,
Until I took my next job not realising it would be my last.
It was on a farm in Wiltshire with lots and lots of cows –
Pet rabbits, cats, dogs and horses all except for sows!
I knew the minute I met them
with their children sat on settee
And the tiny baby wrapped in blanket –

this was the job for me.
The house was really massive
with a walk-in airing cupboard with light,
Which was lovely and warm for feeding the baby,
especially in the night.
Over a period of many months
of carrying children on hip,
I'd encountered a searing pain in my legs,
which was giving me the jip.
This stiffness in my legs and pain
would start without warning,
And almost made it impossible
to walk first thing in the morning.
But good old Ibuprofen, it worked for me every time
And after several days it was gone and I was fine.
It was during this time in the summer
that I visited the family before,
While eating our lunch with the telly on
it shocked us what we saw.
A man had randomly gone round Hungerford
shooting with a gun
And slowly walking up the street
he shot people one by one.
It's one of those days I shall always remember,
you never forget what you see
It's the sort of thing that only happens
to people in films on TV.
But back to reality and down on the farm,

The summer was here with a blast,
As the combines were making their way across fields
It reminded me of my past.
With little one sat on the back of my bike
We would whiz to the farm down the hill,
And singing aloud and with aeroplane arms
I'd remind her to sit very still!
The Spring of 86, was a happy time for me,
I married Chris in our village church
and the locals all came to see.
It was the wedding you see in books,
it was like a fairy-tale,
As the organist played my favourite song
'A Whiter Shade of Pale'.
It was around this time I'd been to the doctor
and had my regular smear,
But as weeks went on and I'd heard no news –
the results I began to fear.
It appeared my irregular cells had gone berserk,
and not knowing,
And the prospect of cervical cancer
was an issue that was ever-growing,
And after the treatment I rested, for several weeks in bed –
Hardly my head I was nursing,
it was my nether regions instead!
As time ticked on a growing concern
was that we couldn't conceive a child,
With the constantly trying both day and night

was beginning to drive us both wild.
The next thing Chris did was the specimen part –
I can look back now and laugh,
But for those of you out there who've been down this road
It's not taken lightly by half.
But lucky for us it all went to plan,
And while sitting upstairs on the loo,
I remember it well –
The pregnancy test that turned from a pink to a blue.
I loved being pregnant it suited me well,
As mint sauce and Snickers did too,
And even today my car door will show
All the wrappers – as there are a few.
Again that dreaded time was looming,
The sad goodbyes had come,
But this time it was different
I was going to be the mum.
I only had a week to go before this babe was due.
My bags were packed and house was straight,
but when it would come who knew.
I was sitting on the edge of my bed
and having a little think,
"These bedroom walls I thought were dull –
I think I'll paint them pink."
So back from town I trundled with tin of paint in hand,
And began to paint our bedroom walls
while on the stool did stand.
It didn't take me long and Chris was away all day,

What a lovely surprise I thought it would be
I wonder what he'll say?
I covered his eyes with my hands and said,
"Tell me, what do you think"?
He gasped and laughing said – "It's psychedelic pink!"
My walls became a talking point
when everyone came to see
Our beautiful boy who was born,
a few days later just in time for tea.
There are no words that can ever describe
that feeling of being a mum,
I couldn't believe I'd produced this baby
I'd carried nine months in my tum.
He was close beside my bed in a cot,
I couldn't have him out of sight,
And that overwhelming excited feeling
kept me awake for most of the night.
Adam was a sheer delight – the perfect baby too,
And was called the Milky Bar kid as he grew a little older,
with glasses and eyes that were blue.
His Nanny would see him daily
and would baby-sit on the occasional night,
Where we'd go out and have a few drinks –
inevitably it would end in a fight.

Labour

It's ten past one in the morning this really is insane,
I'm not sure why I've woken up I think I had a pain.
So I wriggle down the bed it's the middle of the night,
Half an hour later – again, I knew I'd got it right.
That little niggly pain was definitely there in tum,
"Wake up Chris its coming, I'm going to be a mum."
I put my bags by the door and quickly ran a bath,
I think Chris thought I'd have it then and said,
"You're having a laugh".
I closely timed the pain cos in between I knew
I had to quickly do the things that only I could do.
We slowly made the journey, to Swindon in the car,
Contractions every twenty minutes I hope it wasn't far.
I was taken into a little room and got up on the bed,
And laid there looking at the clock, 3.40 that it read.
Breakfast came and went, I drifted in and out of sleep,
And the straps across my tummy hurt
and the machine did constantly bleep.
The pain was really revving up
and the injection in my thigh,
Cupped together with the gas and air –
I was really on a high.
The pain was just unbearable,
I wanted to scream and shout,
But as my sister nicely put it

"What's in has gotta come out!"
The pain had reached crescendo point
it must be nearly through,
The nurse said I must really push
on the count of one and two.
If pushing was my lifeline I'm telling you right now,
I pushed for England with all my might
and sounded like a cow!
The waiting game was over, I'd breezed it with no hitches,
Though my language was a little blue
as they sorted out my stitches!

***

And Then...

After having Adam I encountered monthly pain,
That would double me over
and I'd roll on the floor –
something I couldn't explain.

I eventually saw the doctor
who sent me for an op –
where endometriosis was discovered,
another thing I seemed to cop.

The pain was so bad I was given a course of drugs
that would help me get through –
but my left buttock went numb and I grew extra hairs
which alarmed me, to mention a few.

So trying to conceive again
was even harder than before,
and the prospect of getting pregnant again
seemed to slip through open doors.

But lo and behold on a November morning
I started to feel unwell,
my period was late – my boobs were sore,
I was pregnant I knew I could tell.

And so the maternity wardrobe came out,
big dresses and trousers I wore
that slowly expanded their fullest extent
till there wasn't the room for no more.

My tummy grew quite rapidly
and sleeping I did not –
those size 12 jeans were distant memories
I'd almost quite forgot.

The flat we lived in was lovely
and the baby's room
I have to say was really sweet and cosy
and ready for it any day.

Thursday August 12th – I'd given Adam his tea,
Chris was doing taxi runs, a really busy bee.
I'd had a twinge at lunchtime and I recognised it to be
the start of labour was coming round second time for me.

Again the suitcase was ready,
packed at the top of the stairs,
but Chris wasn't anywhere to be found
he was dashing about taking fares.

My family turned up for moral support,
my sister couldn't believe what it was like –
me pacing the floor waiting for Chris
and my dad went home in a fright.

The pain was intense as we headed in car
for the Norfolk and Norwich it was then,
as we reached the front gates I glanced at my watch
and saw it was quarter past ten.

I remember the rain as I banged my head
and my hair slide shot under my door,

I then grovelled around on my hands and my knees
Chris was fearful I'd have it on floor.

It was all very quiet on delivery ward
I was the only one there I could see,
and Ann was born, on Friday 13th –
unlucky for some but not me.

This wonderful babe beside me in cot
I just couldn't love any more,
and smiling I remember the talk the nurse gave
to make sure there's not any more!

Unbeknown to me the day she was born
her Great Gran had died the same day,
they say one soul dies another is born
and for our family that was the way.

Our bundle of joy was an absolute delight
and people would stop me and say –
how beautiful she was, I should enter her in 'Baby Boots'
she'd win hands down all the way.

So enter I did and lo and behold
the words of the public came true –
our baby did win the Boots competition
and made us such proud parents too.

As the children got bigger the taxis did too
and my sister still driving for us,
decided it would be fancy dress for New Year's Eve,
this wasn't an option – a must!

We had Father Christmas, an Arab,
a belly dancer and Superman to name just a few,
but the shock was my sister who came as a Monk –
I can tell you she turned the air blue!

It was totally shocking,
she found a bald wig and managed to stubble a beard,
you should've seen the look on everyone's faces,
she looked scary and totally weird.

It was during this time the shop below the flat
was vacant and free,
to be snapped up by a shop owner,
and the one that was next was me.

I'd always wanted a coffee shop,
to produce everything that's homemade,
with pretty tablecloths and lovely china –
not all modern, minimalistic and staid.

And so it was, I owned one
and called it 'The Coffee Pot',
and bought the china and crockery –
my god there seemed a lot.

The decor was pretty in blue and yellow
and we soon built it up with a name,
of having the most delicious scones
that returned people again and again.

It was on this particular morning
I was carrying the soup from the door,

when I tripped and skidded about
till I belly-danced and fell on the floor.

Minestrone soup when cold
isn't a good look to be fair,
and even less appealing
when dripping from one's hair!

I seemed to fly just everywhere
across the coffee machine,
I was trying not to make a noise
in case the lady in the corner might've seen.

But these were happy times for me
though long and hard hours too,
that took me away from my children at times –
luckily there were only a few.

The children were slowly growing
and we were bulging out of the seams,
till we found a cottage in Ryburgh,
it was undoubtedly the house of my dreams.

It was incredibly old with a wheel in the wall
that had obviously belonged to a cart,
and with beams in the ceiling and interior brickwork,
I loved it, it was old and yet smart.

I painstakingly decorated Ann's room first
with a wallpaper checked yellow and blue,
with a frieze of cream ducks that waddled along
just above her cot that was new.

But this wasn't to be, on her first morning she woke,
I was gutted when I walked in and saw,
all the duck frieze had taken a fly,
she'd ripped it and they were all on the floor.

Chris's mum Doreen was diagnosed with leukaemia
and so it was decided that we –
would have her live out her life in the care of our home
and be nursed to the end by me.

With my marriage so bad and God rest her soul
I really did give it my best,
and caring for elderly people you know,
certainly put all my skills to their test.

Life without Doreen was empty at first,
she'd always been there for me –
to patch up the fights that were caused by her son,
she knew we'd divorce, she told me.

We took her ashes to be buried in Inkpen
and she travelled on my lap in the car,
the journey seemed endless;
it really was a long way by far.

The decision was made that she'd be buried
in the gap that was there you could see,
but don't ask me what happened,
Rosie observed that they'd dug a hole under a tree!

So during the service unbeknown to us
she'd given the undertaker a spade,

and got him to re-dig a new hole for her
that had been earmarked in the space that was made.

Having just buried Doreen
bad news kept ringing in my ears,
my mum said that Dad's cells had changed
and with cancer they gave him a year.

So with an operation and chemotherapy later,
the specialist had told us no lie,
Mum nursed him at home, we would all be around
for the time when we knew he would die.

How hard was that to watch your own dad
have his life slowly taken away,
I will never forget how peaceful it was –
"Thank you" whoever for making it that way.

So with two parents gone a decision was now made
that really gave me no choice
and I'm a great believer that we all have the ability
but don't listen to our own inner voice.

As time ticked on oblivious to outsiders
but so very obvious to me,
my marriage had ended I could stick it no more,
a divorce in the distance could see.

So without too much detail as it still wrenches my heart,
no divorce is ever easy they say,
but the Decree Absolute came through two years later,
on the morning of the second of May.

I knew I was right to divorce Chris
so I moved out to live with my mum,
a difficult time for me all round,
but for now it was just number one.

I look back now and wonder
how did I cope with no children, no home and no money,
and the signing on weekly cos my work came to a halt,
was demoralising and really not funny.

But time is a healer and you DO have to cope
even when money is thin,
and like I said earlier you have two choices in life –
you can either sink or you swim.

So I picked myself up and slowly
moved on with a hysterectomy now under my belt.
That took me months to get over that
with everything else that I felt.

The morning of the first of October –
another I remember with dread –
the phone call of my hysterical mother to say
Chris had hung himself and was dead.

It was one of those poignant moments
when I just didn't know what to do,
did I cry, make a coffee, do the washing up
even hoovering – who knew.

All I knew was my children would need me
and for one going round in his head was that

he'd blame me for leaving his father,
and now his father was dead.

I know I had divorced him
and I'd moved on with a brand-new life,
but I loved him still for twenty-three years
and was married to him as his wife.

I'm back at my job working again
with children and babies I love,
a turbulent past,
even I will agree as I re read the pages above.

I continue to write as my life is now fun
and you will read what's been happening to me,
and I hope that you'll have as much fun
going through it as I smile cos its all about me!

***

This is the history part about me, and after this there is obviously a long period of time which I didn't feel needed recording, or to a certain extent, even remembering.

So the next poems are situations that have happened to me, and yes, they really have happened.

Our Trip to Vegas

An early start it was for us,
the frost lay on the ground,
We crept around the house a lot,
not daring to make a sound.
We packed into the minibus,
the atmosphere was sad,
Then Anne squawked,
"Don't go just yet,
I forgot to get my bag."
The airport it was busy,
with people to and fro
All we really wanted was
to get the plane and go.
Grant was buying aftershave,
and potions for the showers,
Till suddenly the tannoy announced,
"Delayed for several hours"
Well that was it; we took our seats,
our faces to the floor
And sat quite near a minging family,
of four or five or more.
'The Benefit lot' you know the scene,
all gobby rings and gold
But what caught our eyes was loner boy,
who didn't look too old,

A little tear he started to shed,
us thinking his flight he'd missed,
In fact the problem with him
was he was thoroughly and utterly pissed.
But the lady in the green top, little did she know,
a shoulder for him to cry on
He would never let her go.
She patted his shoulder, rubbed his back,
as he sat next to her in his seat
Until he suddenly stood no more,
and collapsed on her lap in a heap.
The burgers we had eaten had really saved the day,
though unfortunately the flight was long,
and we farted all the way.

Our hotel was amazing,
with rows and rows of slots,
Of people walking round,
with huge big plastic pots.
An early night was needed,
we were exhausted from the flight,
We unpacked our clothes, jumped into bed,
and swiftly said, "Goodnight."
The jetlag it's a killer, and took us days to wake,
And we walked the earth to find the shops –
boy, did our feet ache.
The Starbucks girl she knew us well,
we were there sharp at seven
For irresistible coffee,
we died and went to heaven.
Amazing what you crave,
at four o'clock in morning,
When woken by the sound
of Grant and Anne snoring.
The shops they were amazing,
with everything to buy,
And only I could get collared,
by a dodgy make up guy,
Who sat me down and told me,
that there was no hope for me,
But if I bought a tub of anti-aging cream,
I'd get another free!

We came to the Bellagio,
the fountains they were great,
You don't have to squash to see them,
as people stand around and wait.
And with anticipation,
camera poised and bag in hand,
I tripped and landed with a splat,
and nosedived to the ground.
I laughed so much I couldn't see,
and didn't want to make a fuss,
And Anne said to Grant
"Ignore her, we'll pretend she's not with us."
We headed for the Forum, a shopping centre too,
With lots of shops and candy stalls,
and plenty of things to do.
But getting there was quite a feat,
as a smell shot up our noses
My god, it made you gag,
cause that weren't no smell of roses!
Having passed the heaving smell,

which frankly was quite shitty,
We headed for Anne's favourite shop,
oh yes, it's Hello Kitty.
With such a choice and so many gifts,
to buy all in one day,
We bought our things,
thanked the girl who said "Happy Holiday."
We caught the escalator, to the food hall at the top,
where the choice was overwhelming,
and we didn't know where to stop...
Until the Chinese counter where the lady with the stick,
Held something out for us, I said,
"This should do the trick."
"What is it?" questioned Grant,
it looked a lump of mess.
"I'm not sure I should eat that,
it'll give me IBS."
We all had the chicken something,
and tasty it was too
Though quite how long will it be,
before we all need the loo?

The Canyon trip was booked,
we awoke around five o'clock
We queued up for the shower,
the hour it was a shock.
The minibus it turned up sharp,
to take us on our trip,
And the driver stuck his right foot down,

and drove like a lunatic.
We arrived at the airport,
excitement in our heads,
When the Chinese girl said
"Fright is cancelled, all go back to bed."
Anne said, "That's great, so what do we all do now?
She could have told us earlier, the drippy, silly cow."
So back we trundled to our room,
tail between our legs,
And we did as the Chinese girl suggested,
and crawled back into bed.
We didn't do the trip, what more is there to say,
The weather was atrocious,
and we were going home the next day.
Anne and I had an early night, as Grant went to a show,
So we slowly packed our things away,
as tomorrow we would go.
Next door seemed to be having a party,
and the noise it did exceed,
But lingering in the air, oh no,
was the smell of stinking weed.
If the stench got any stronger, for us it should be said,
That we will sleep like logs, and when Grant gets in
He'll think that we are dead.
We packed our bags and journeyed on,
the flight again was long,
But with ear plugs in, and music loud,
we hummed our way till home.

My Pressie from My Sister

I was sitting in New York,
with a friend whom I adore,
Who'd treated me to Niagara Falls,
I'd never been there before.
It was a birthday to remember,
and fond memories I have well,
But awaiting the pressie from my sister,
is a story I must tell.
She lives in Arizona,
and rang me on the day,
Hey Mary, she said, Happy Birthday,
your pressie's on its way.
So down to reception I toddled,
and asked the lady if she'd had,
An envelope from Arizona,
in a fairly large brown bag.
She sent me down to luggage,
which was down along corridor,
Where sat on a stool
was a big black chap, called Doug,
He'd help me for sure.
I told him it was my birthday,
and a pressie was coming to me,
I gave my name and room number,
which I think was 4143.

He checked and nothing had come,
and said to call back in an hour
And with diamond in ear, and shiny white teeth
He smiled and said, "See you then flower."
So back I returned to Doug on his stool
Who was waiting for people to arrive,
Again I gave him my name and my room,
Which I think was 4145.
Confusion was now slowly setting in,
as my room wasn't booked in my name
And my pressie my sister had sent me,
was sent in my old maiden name
"You sure you are who you are?" said Doug,
this has all got confusing to me
First you're one name, then you're another,
and your room's 415 and not 3.
"Of course it's me," I said,
though I really didn't know what to do
And behind me some people had gathered,
and slowly had formed a long queue.
I was getting all hot round the collar,
and my birthday was going all wrong
'Come on Doug, what do you want me to do? ' I said –

"Tap dance or sing you a song?"
And much to my horror he said "Yes,
I think that would be just fine…"
So I sang Whitney Houston and took a deep breath,
And belted out 'One Moment in Time'.
Doug was roaring with laughter,
teeth beaming from ear to ear
And after what seemed like eternity,
the crowd had started to cheer.

"Man, you got some lungs on you,"
he said on his stool, with his hands on his lap
But I had a job to hear him,
as the crowd had started to clap.

It really was hilarious,
when all I went there to get,
Was my pressie from my sister,
which still hadn't got there yet.

We had to leave the next day,
and we were waiting, as you do,
When the hotel receptionist said to me,
"There's a parcel here waiting for you."
I thanked her for coming to get me,
as we were rushing to catch out jet,
"NO thank YOU' she said 'for entertaining us."
This parcel we'll never forget.

A miracle!

Lucky or unlucky,
Whichever way you view
I wear the daily contact lenses
And they cost a bob or two.
And in the daytime I find,
My glasses I wear best,
And when the nighttime comes around
My eyes have had a rest.
Now I know this sounds ridiculous
And I'm sure it doesn't happen to most,
But without my glasses or lenses in,
I'm as blind and as deaf as a post.
But on this particular evening
At the Christmas party thing,
I'd had one too many drinks
And the room began to swing.
We'd got a taxi home (of course)
And up the stairs I went,
Undressed and flopped right into bed
A good night had was spent.
I woke in the morning and while sitting on the loo,
I grabbed the seat, you see –
I really thought that God had turned
A miracle on me.
Everything was in detail,

The bottles on the shelf were clear,
"Chris," I yelled "get out of bed,
And get yourself in here."
"I can see, I can see it's a miracle."
Until Chris laughed and said,
"You forgot to take your lenses out
When you stumbled into bed!"
I think there's a little lesson here
To you all who have a few,
Take your lenses out at night,
Or you'll think God's blessed you too!

***

Cold Sores

Oh my God I've got a cold sore,
It came up last night in bed,
It woke me up this morning
Really throbbing in my head.
I looked in bathroom mirror
And all that I could see
Was a monumental carbuncle
Staring back at me.
It starts off as a blister,
Which doesn't look that much,
But because it throbs and hurts a lot
The temptation's there to touch.
The biggest problem that I find
Is shopping – it's a task,
Of dodging people that I know –
I'd love to wear a mask.

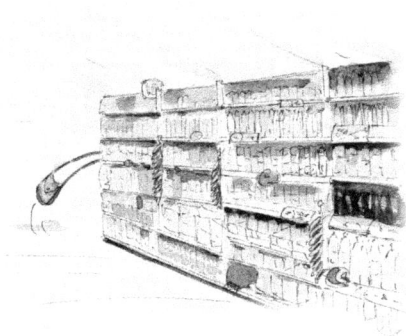

Inevitably you'll meet someone
While nipping out right quick,
And the minute you start talking,
Their eyes zoom in on my lip.
I try to be polite
And don't have much to say,
'cos all I want them to do
Is go and walk away.
I completely lose my confidence
And socialising is a 'NO',
Why the hell can't cold sores design themselves
To come up on one's toe!
My daughter said, "Oh Mummy,
You really look a sight,
You can't go out with that on your lip,
You'll give everyone a fright."
I've tried the creams and plasters,
I've put them to the test,
But a little dab of oven cleaner,
I find it works the best.
I'm seriously not joking,
And I'm sure it shouldn't be,
That oven cleaner on your lip
Should work – but it did for me.
I came across it just by chance,
When I opened the cupboard door,
And the oven cleaner accidentally
Landed on the floor.

I'm sure that health and safety,
Would have something to say,
But who cares if it is oven cleaner
That makes it go away!

The Chip Van

I used to live in Ryburgh a village not so far,
That sometimes has a bus service,
so you need a reliable car.
It has a lovely pub and a local village shop,
But the highlight was a Friday
when the chip van it would stop.
We all walked down, but on this day
I decided to take the car,
As fifty yards just down the road
To me seemed way too far.
Quite a crowd had gathered
And they chattered and talked with ease,
I put in my order for cod and chips,
Five-eighty if you please.
I said goodbye, sat down to drive home
Even though it wasn't so far,

"My god" I said, "I'm sorry."
And I didn't know his name,
It was dark and to be quite frank
All the cars just looked the same.
I apologised profusely
As I'm sure it seemed quite shocking
And I looked up and saw the crowd was laughing,
And the chip van it was rocking.
An easy mistake to make, anyone can see,
But why is it that things seem to always happen to me!

***

The Man on the Bike

When the children were young they went to Colkirk,
A village school over the hill,
Which was handy close and nearby
Should the occasion arise they were ill.
On this particular day
I set off to collect them at three
In plenty of time to chat to the mums
About gossip that was handed out free.
But as I drove to the top of the hill
I could see this pushbike ahead,
Parked on its stand on the side of the road,
And a man that was scratching his head.
I pulled up behind the bike
And the man that was German had found,
A pheasant that wasn't quite dead
And flapping about on the ground.
This clearly was upsetting this man
Who had cameras and bags on his back,
And was in a right state when I stopped,
He was not in the mood for a chat.
The man was anxious to help it,
And I could see had a tear in his eye,
But I explained that the pheasant was injured,
And was on its way out and would die.
But this man seemed so highly strung

And eccentric I would say,
So I figured he was best left alone
And I decided to get on my way.
I started my car, I could see him,
His arms in the air what a sight,
Which is just as well he was occupied,
'Cos I drove forward and ran over his bike.
I stopped and reversed backwards
Surely now he would've looked up,
But no, he was so wrapped up
with the pheasant in his arms,
Which now he began to rock.
I would never leave the scene of an accident
But I felt on this particular day,
It was best to leave this man on his own,
So again I set off on my way.
But as I looked back in my mirror
On his bike with the bird to his chest,
His handlebars were pointing eastwards,
And his wheel seemed to turn to the west!
Steve Wright at this time had a radio show
Where people would ring in and be
Sorry for doing the things that they'd done,
I should've rung in,as one of them was me!

***

Apologies to man whoever you are – I hope you got home
alright!

The New Year's Eve Kiss

We owned a taxi company for many years you see,
Where drivers came and went,
and then it was down to me.
It was getting close to midnight,
the lull before the storm,
We were sat in the office, drinking tea,
When suddenly in walked 'Norm'.
Quite smartly dressed I'd say, and shoes with pointed toes,
And a kindly face with brushed back hair,
And a ring right through his nose.
"I don't suppose there's any chance," he said,
"of taking me –
Just quickly home?
The fastest route and pretty much for free."
He staggered round and got in car,
oh no I think he's pissed,
And leaned across and loudly said,
"Any chance of a New Year's kiss?"
"Sit back," I said, "and belt yourself in,"
I thought that would do the trick,
But his head rolled back,
"I'm sorry love but I think I'm gonna be sick."
With brakes slammed on, and seatbelt off,
he chundered in his hand,
I opened the door, and pushed him out,

and he landed on the ground.
He hit his head and rolled around,
spluttering and being sick,
Looked up at me with bleeding nose, and said
"That's done the trick."
My uttermost priority was to get this bugger home,
Who stank of sick, and wandering hands
had started slowly roam.
"I'm really sorry lovey," he said, "I know I've been a pain,
But I really think you're lovely – Norman is my name."
We turned the corner, house in sight,
just time for him to pay,
He tipped me well, and turned around,
and had something to say,
"We nearly didn't make it, and the chimes I'd hate to miss,
But I don't suppose there's any chance
I could have my New Year's kiss!"

***

Dinner Round Some Friends

Another excellent night round yours, the table was a scene,
And food as always just delicious, and fit to feed a queen.
The chef is quite dynamic and grows his own veg too,
– though I gather the cat had left her mark,
beside them with a poo!
I know you can't repeat this
and you'll have to keep it quiet,
But as we sat round table waiting,
in the kitchen there seemed a riot.
The chocolate for the fondue
had given up and all gone thick,
So quickly I tipped some water in
and it seemed to do the trick.
But the problem wasn't the chocolate
and the lack of it was sad,
"Well, I tipped the first lot in the bin," said Chris,
"there it is in the bottom of the bag."

So with no adieu the hand went in
and grabbed the soggy lump
all covered in strawberry bits – that'll do
and it went in the bowl with a thump.
With lots of whisking and added cream
it slowly went to thick,
A final dash of amaretto liqueur had really done the trick.
So taking it to the table their faces you should've seen,
It went down with a storm
and we licked our lips right clean.
Thank you for inviting me –
it's difficult as I'm on my own –
but I know you all so well now,
So for me it's home from home.

***

This was actually a thank you card I wrote and sent to some friends who did dinner. A good time is ALWAYS had when I go round theirs, and the food is just fabulous it was just the most hilarious evening and again. "Yes" it really did happen, and thank you for having me – also apologies to everyone else that didn't have a clue what was going on!!

The Taxi Fare to Cromer Hospital

It was a late November morning
that I had a taxi fare,
To take a lady to Cromer Hospital,
which was beyond Holt somewhere.
Not knowing where I was going
we left in plenty of time,
To allow for 'getting lost' –
the appointment was at half past nine.
I parked outside her house,
and tooted on the horn,
Out she came with her purple rinse,
and a woolly coat, well worn.
She was a lovely little old lady,
and chatted all the way,
And interesting to talk to,
I could have listened to her all day.
I'd gone through Cromer High Street,
twice, but the hospital I couldn't find,
And with time ticking on,
and feeling slightly panicky,
I thought I was going out of my mind.
Somebody said "It's easy,
it's up the hill on the left, set back."
So I drove into what I thought was it,
and out walked a man in a white mac.

He had a hat on, gloves and boots,
all matching in white too,
And slowly walked towards me, and said,
"Hello, can I help you?"
And, "Yes," I said, "I hope so,
I'm trying to find the hospital."
By now two other men came out,
and all three started to giggle.
They gave me great directions
and sent me on my way,
But curiosity got the better of me,
and I turned and said, "I say –
what exactly is this place?"
And looking at all three men –
"Well lovey, you come her to catch it,
and you go to hospital to rid of 'em!"
So feeling none the wiser,
and foolish now perhaps –
I'd only pulled into a factory,
that was famous for Cromer crabs!!
I simply burst out laughing,
and went on my merry way,
And left the three men laughing,
cause I knew I'd made their day.

***

Henny Penny

We kept a lot of chickens,
and they laid eggs for the shop,
Forty-eight a day I'd get,
it never seemed to stop.
Every day they'd be collected,
and as I toddled down the garden,
I'd be followed by this little one,
who'd cluck "I beg your pardon."
She must fly over the top of the fence,
I could never work it out,
And leave the others all behind, shouting
"Oi come get us out."
I'd be cooking in the kitchen,
when I'd hear a tap on the door,
And every day she'd knock and stand there
waiting on the floor.
She became part of the family,
and came in every day,
And sat with the dogs and rabbit asleep,
and the kids' friends they would say –
"I wish we had a chicken you could cuddle,
it's well cool."
I'm sure though when people saw it
they must have thought 'damn fool'.
But everybody knew her, including the cockerel

who lived next door
She disappear with him for hours,
I can't imagine what she went there for!
I'd only have to call her in my Henny Penny voice,
She always come back home to me,
I was glad as it was her choice.
As with all laying chickens,
their sell by date had come –
They had to go for – well whatever –
or even another home.
And luckily we knew a man
that kept chickens running free
"I've got hundreds of 'em in a field," he said,
"they can come and live with me"
The idea was terrific,
and he told me what he'd do,
Collect them when it's dark,
so there won't be a hullaballoo.
I felt tipped Henny Penny's wings in black s
o he would know
That she was rather special
and was definitely not to go.
So with the task done, the very next morning,
I heard a crying from my son –
"Mummy you've got to do something,
they've taken the wrong one."
And sure enough there sat one chicken,
perched by the shed door,

On close examination,
no felt tip marks I saw.
So with a box and lots of straw,
I made my way in car,
To the place where Henny Penny lived,
I knew it wasn't far.
They lived in a mobile home,
which was parked beside a fence,
And as I slowly started walking,
the chickens did commence.
The field had simply hundreds,
and they all looked just the same,
And I bet none of them would come when called,
or had a special name,
A lady came to greet me,
she had short grey curly hair,
And said "You'll never find her, my booty,
there are hundreds that are there."
So I waded my way through them,
and shouted out her name,
I could see the lady thinking –
daft bat, she's gone insane.
As I slowly walked towards the car,
calling out her name,
I turned and saw her charging towards me,
like a runaway express train.
She followed me back to the car,
where I opened the passenger door,

The lady stood there shaking her head,
saying "I've never seen the likes before."
She was a darling chicken,
and she really DID know her name,
She even came to school one day,
as she became incredibly tame.
But it's while we were away on holiday,
I remember it cause I cried,
The phone call came to tell us
that my Henny Penny had died.
She's had a turn and was wandering round the garden,
maybe looking round for me
But I'd left strict instructions
that she be buried under the tree.
So for all of you that read this,
and think it sounds insane –
Remember that even chickens
do sometimes have a brain.

**

This next poem was written when I was not in a good place just after Chris died, and for me having to go to the job centre was just the worst thing in the world, it makes you feel so useless, worthless and for me I felt cheated – I was jogging along nicely and then I was put into a situation that stopped everything, and having to sit there – wanting to work and couldn't and having to rely on handouts – something I never ever thought I would have to do. It was just hideous and I have to say what a fantastic system we have because there IS the help out there for people like me who at the time really did need it and those people at the job centre could not have been nicer and gave me the temporary help that I needed – "Thank you." And this next poem was just one of those days I remembered.

Sitting at the Job Centre.

It became a weekly thing –
a chore and what a task,
To sit and wait in the job centre
where they'd tediously ask
If you'd tried to look for work,
which was impossible for me,
As I tried to sort some money out
that was handed out for free.
But sitting right beside me
on such a particular day
was a well-built man with stubble on his face –
quite dashing I would say!
I sat and listened while she questioned him about his work
as she wrote on the page,
And he sadly replied,
"There's not much call for a crane driver now
in this day and age."
I think he would have spoken
if the lady hadn't caught my eye,
Which is just as well as looking back
I was quiet then and very shy.
This man walked out and looked as though
he had the world upon his shoulders,
You'd never think by looking at him
his job was moving boulders.

So I sat and listened while the kindly lady
tried to sort me out,
And further down some dodgy guy
had begun to scream and shout.
Those tedious days are passed now for me,
but not for many of you,
My advice is – get a job, they're out there,
all be it at the moment a few.

***

Feeling Low

As I'm sitting by the window
with my parrot on her stand,
My stomach, shoulders, body hurts
as I rest my head in hands.
If you ask me how I feel – I don't know,
can't say I'm not sick,
And normally a couple of tablets
would certainly do the trick.
I have an anxious feeling,
that's in my stomach deep,
That wakes me in the middle of the night,
and prevents me going to sleep.
Maybe I am hungry, I think,
and eat some more cooked ham,
But the feeling doesn't go away,
it's like you get before an exam.
This is the first time in my life,
that I haven't actually worked,
And not being round children and babies,
is driving me berserk.
I feel so utterly useless,
sitting here and feeling blue,
There must be something out there,
with children, that I can do.
I now have my daughter Anne with me,

which is absolutely great,
Any work that would jeopardise her stability,
I couldn't do and she would hate.
I got the forms of 'foster caring' –
I could help children in their plight,
"You'd be perfect," said the lady,
"though the timing isn't right"
I struggle at the moment,
it's like a continual song,
Of not knowing how to pay the bills,
or where the next penny's coming from.
But you have to think positive,
as my father always said,
"Never look behind you –
always look ahead."
And as my parrot makes me smile,
I find it all very scary,
She whistles and laughs exactly like me,
and says, "Looking good Mary."

***

Pain

However can I manage to sleep,
this really is insane,
My Ankylosing Spondylitis
has reared its head again
I have it in my hips
and half way up my spine,
And apart from the occasional tweak,
I haven't had pain for some time.
It comes on with no warning,
this time while getting out of the car,
And prevents me from walking normally,
thank god Argos isn't far.
I had to try and focus,
to walk as normally as can be,
Bu the pain is so excruciating,
and people do start to look at me.
There isn't any pain I think,
that comes as close as this,
Why me? I sometimes wonder.
Is God just taking the piss?
No ibuprofen or paracetamol
will even touch the pain,
And it makes me just so irritable,
and there's no one I can blame.
I went to see the doctor,

and explained the pain and said,
"I just can't get about,
and even roll over in my bed."
I've now been given painkillers,
and steroids to name a few,
So hopefully in time, I'll be pain free,
to eventually make the loo.
And as I'm slowly writing,
it's like a weight lifting from my head
And the pain is now going,
and I can move about in bed.
I wonder what tomorrow will bring,
and how the pain will be
I'm going to sleep,
cause for now I can,
and I'm just about pain free.

***

The Marriage Proposal

While going through my divorce
I worked in a dress shop in Lynn,
Selling wedding dresses to would-be brides
That were fat, short, tall and some thin.
But with this job came a Smart Car,
in bright pink – you should see,
And written all over in thick black writing
read, no less than 'Bride 2 Be'.
So on this particular morning
I needed to stop off for fuel,
And noticed the car pull beside me
And got out was a man that was tall.
He stared and was reading the writing,
Unmistakably read 'Bride 2 Be',
And with twinkle in eye and bright green jumper,
He came over and went down on one knee.
I was taken aback when I saw him
and it took me a minute or two to ask,
"What on earth are you doing?" He replied –
"You're gorgeous – will you?"
I just couldn't grasp what was happening
Till I saw him read 'Bride 2 Be' –
Good God this man was crackers,
And was only proposing to me!
I just didn't know what to do

In a situation as random as this,
And the mood that this man was now in,
Might've planted my lips with a kiss.
So being the blonde, I squashed his pride
And really put on the dampers,
And said, "Look I'm sorry young man,
but it has to be said,
That I just don't like men in green jumpers!".
I ran in to pay and hurry to work,
If only my boss really knew –
What chaos this car is causing me,
'Bride 2 Be' – cos it just isn't true!

***

Ann's 16th Birthday Treat

We took a trip to London
The music, Ann simply adores,
It's the *Lion King* it's amazing,
I've seen it six times before!
I thought it would be nice for her
So Jed he came in tow,
And with bags packed and with Cilla (satnav)
Off to London we did go.
I've never driven in London
So for me it was a first,
To meet the hustle, bustle, of road rage drivers,
My language! I thought would burst.
Cilla did a fine job
Till we reached a roundabout,
And she kept on saying *"Turn left, turn left!"*
We couldn't! and she seemed to shout.
I was getting hot a flustered
And got wedged between a bus,
And a lorry with a driver
who ranted, swore and cussed.
The conversation with Cilla
was getting me just nowhere,
till suddenly we turned down a road?
At last, I think we're there.
We stayed with Gus in Battersea,

A long-term friend of mine,
Who gave up his bed and spare room,
To sofa it, which he said was fine.
Jed had brought some glow sticks
Which were colourful, luminous and bright,
And came in pretty handy
In the middle of the night.
I slept in a double bed
Which was built four feet off the floor,
That had draws and extra storage
Which was handy, that's for sure.
So I'd got myself tucked into bed
With my ear plugs in for the night,
And was woken by what I thought was a burglar
And it gave me quite a fright.
I wasn't really with it
Though my heart by now was pounding,
And in the background, I could hear Ann's voice
"Mum, Mum" – it just kept sounding.
Till eventually I sat bolt upright
And glanced towards the door, –
There stood I thought a ghost,
With glow sticks near the floor.
Now you have to remember here.
That without glasses it's all a blur,
And no matter how hard I tried
Ann didn't look like her.
What with me screaming out of fright,

I sat upright in bed,
And not realising where I was,
I really smacked my head.
Gus by now had appeared
To reassure us that the noise was fine –
It was foxes in the bins next door
which happened all the time.
And sure enough when we looked out the window,
A fox next door we could see,
Chomping on last night's leftovers!!!
Another nice meal that was free.

***

Losing weight

As I'm standing in the mirror – naked,
looking at myself,
I'm not surprised I haven't got a man,
I'll end up on the shelf.
Everything seems to have got bigger,
Well everything except my mouth,
And it seems to wobble more and droop,
Even my kneecaps are heading south!
My trousers are too tight
And I seem to have a ledge,
Where I can pick the waistline flab up
And hang it over the edge.
If only there weren't Snicker bars
To tempt me I just know –
The weight would surely drop off
And the inches they would go.
I've tried the cut down bit
And the exercising more,
And even bought an abs machine
That lives behind the door.
I bought the latest DVD
Of club dance and all the moves,
But the jumping up and down was so vigorous,
I nearly knocked myself out with my boobs.
So having been on a diet for...

22 years with no hope,
Just give me a man caked in Snicker bars now –
I could eat all day long – yeh I'd cope!

***

This poem is I'm sure so true to life for a lot of people, and I have come to the conclusion that it really doesn't matter if you are a little bit overweight, it's how you feel inside, and no I'm not the skinniest person on the planet but I'm well and your health is the most important thing of all, and as long as you are healthy that's all that matters 'cos if you haven't got it life doesn't go to plan. I have my aches and pains, which I am rarely without nowadays, but I can deal with that, so yes there are still Snicker wrappers in my car to this day!

My Operation

On Monday morning at quarter to eight,
I was booked in at BUPA for an op,
So I got up at six so as not to be late,
as Norwich was by no means a hop,
I couldn't have breakfast or even a drink,
which included my super ground coffee,
And the op I was having was a pretty big one –
the long overdue hysterectomy.
So we set off in car with my mum at the wheel,
an atmosphere sombre for me,
Stomach all churning with anticipation,
I'll soon be as fit as a flea.
With time ticking on, mum stepped on the gas,
and we shot past a lorry real quick,
When out of the blue the engine went bang,
and I thought I was going to be sick!
We cruised into a layby which luckily was near,
my mum was so stressed I could tell,
"Who on earth can we call at this unearthly hour –
Mick'll help us, we know him so well."
So we sat and we waited till a car pulled in close,
and out stepped a bleary-eyed Mick,
"Good morning ladies, you'd better hop in,
as I've got to get there pretty quick.'
It was one of those scenes that you see in a film,

when you think it won't happen to you,
Having started on four wheels,
we turned the last bend, and I'm telling you
it seemed like just two.
I left them to park as I ran through the doors,
and was given my name and my number,
And I flew to my room where the surgeon was sitting,
waiting calmly and cool as a cucumber.
We had a quick chat as the nurses moved fast,
to prep me in time for theatre,
The surgeon was gone, and my stockings went on,
I felt like a lamb sent for slaughter.
Mick and Mum reappeared, with Mick by the door,
and Mum sat down on the seat,
And I smiled as the nurse said,
"Will your husband be staying?"
as her eyes slowly moved to his feet,
We laughed when we saw his slippers,
no socks, and a tracksuit to complete the look,
"Don't worry said the nurse, you look fine to me,
you'll go down as one in my book."
When I came round I could hear people talking,
though it all seemed to me like a hum,
My eyes wouldn't open and I just couldn't talk,
as their voices all rolled into one.
I was wheeled to my room by a nurse who reminded me,
that an op of my size was no fun,
I was sure she was right by all of the tubes,

at the time seemed to come from my bum!
My epidural in made me numb from the waist,
and I mean down totally down to my feet,
And I frightened myself when my hand caught my leg,
as it felt like a piece of raw meat.
The next two days I remember so well,
the op had caused pain in my spine,
And with constantly rocking to will it away,
I was everything other than fine.
The morphine they gave me kept me awake,
and the walls which I thought were a blue,
Had pictures that moved around in the room,
and bright lights that flashed with them too.
But each day got better, and soon I went home,
and my tummy even still to this day,
Is numb at the bottom, I could have it all pierced…
what fun… what would my mum say!!!!!

***

Buying Petrol

My regular port of call is the station
at Fakenham it's said,
But on this particular occasion
I went to Morrison's instead.
I pulled up along the pump,
it was such a lovely day,
Nozzle in the tank,
then I heard the tannoy say
"Would lady at pump 8
press payment what it's to be."
I stood there waiting aimlessly,
not realising he was talking to me.
Again I pressed the nozzle –
no diesel was coming through,
I looked up at the man at the desk,
who said, "Yes I'm talking to you."
By which time everybody now,
was laughing aloud at me,
"I can't believe," I said,
"that my pump had talked to me."
I didn't realise that you had to press a button two –
Request the type of payment,
either at kiosk or at pump with you.
But there one thing that I can say,
that I couldn't say before

I've now been spoken to by a diesel pump,
and that's never happened, for sure.

***

Having My Tooth Out

I'm terrified of the dentist,
so every time I go,
and she asks me, "Any problems?"
Unless it's bad, it's a definite "NO."
But recently I've had toothache,
And every time I eat,
the pain shoots up in my tooth
And make me jump up in my seat,
So presenting myself in dentist's chair,
and trying not to scream and shout
She peers into my open mouth and says
"It's definitely got to come out."
Knowing just how scared I am
and I thought I was going to weep
She booked me in at Norwich
Where they would gently put me to sleep,
So with no time to argue, I didn't get a say,
The clinic was called immediately
And I was booked in at ten the next day.
I rushed around in the morning, with lots of things to do,
Feed and clean my parrot out, was one to name a few.
The time was pressing on and she was sitting on her stand,
I went to put her back in cage,
and she flew and bit my hand.
She must have senses how scared I was,

As she's joined to me at the hip,
So with no ado I plonked her in,
and she came with me for the trip.
I sat her in the waiting room, it really wasn't right
And she constantly talked saying, "Looking good, Mary,"
Which was a joke cause I looked a sight.
They called me in the surgery,
and as I sat back in my chair,
I could hear her saying, "I can see you"
and the chap said what's going on out there?
Everyone was laughing as she started opera singing,
But the needle had hit my vein by then,
and the room was slowly swinging.
I awoke after what seemed like hours,
and I'm sure I started to moan
The dentist said, "All's gone well, here's your tooth,
you can now make your way back home."
My mother took my left arm with birdcage in her right,
and I staggered out to her waiting car,
I must have looked a sight.
Whatever must they have thought
of the lady with the bird,
Who'd come to have her tooth out,
it really was absurd.

***

When The Car Caught Fire!

It was later in the summer that I booked us tickets to see
Joseph and his Amazing Dreamcoat
there was Ann, a friend and me.
I'd taken Chris's Jag which to me was such a haul,
And without fail at every light it seemed to always stall.
But on this evening spirits were high
as we approached the Theatre Royal,
Unaware to me, the engine had begun to boil.
I pulled into the car park, there seemed a funny smell,
I wound my window down to see,
it was our car I could now tell.
I opened my car door and couldn't see for smoke,
It caught my lungs and made me cough
and Ann began to choke.
There were lots of people round me
but nobody seemed to care
That smoke was billowing out of the engine,
and they just stood around and stared.
With the engine now on fire, I really didn't have time
And grabbed my mobile phone and quickly dialled 999.
The fire engine didn't take long
and turned the corner quick,
And out jumped five young strapping men,
who were stunning hunks – and fit!
I was on the phone to Chris and trying hard to say

That his car was now on fire, but the sirens got in the way.
Eventually he sent a car to pick us up for home,
And so we replayed the story again,
which gave him time to moan.

***

An Interview in Bath and the Postman!

When Norlands moved from Denford Park
to establish themselves in Bath,
I went for a job which was fairly close
so to stop by, it was in my path.
I'd had a week with a newborn babe
which their benefits of me they did reap,
Though I'm always the one that leaves
looking like death cos of lack of sleep!
So on this particular day
before the journey home I'd embark,
I thought I'd stop off for a sandwich and drink
which I did and pulled over to park.
The sun was shining down on my car,
hotting up as I sat in my seat,
And opened my drink and peeled back
my sarnies of tuna, I started to eat.

With drink between thighs and mouth full of food
I nodded off as quick as a flash,
And was startled by a loud knock on the window,
and was faced with a man with a tache.
My drink wet my seat and I spat out my food,
the shock had caused me to choke,
I wound down my window to a startled young postman,
who thought I had died of a stroke!
"As long as you're ok," he said with a smile,"
I was worried as your head had slumped down."
But I could see by my wet patch
that had now marked my jeans
his eyes looked at me with a frown.
He went on his way when he knew I was fine
and I looked at myself in disgrace,
What must I have looked like
when he tapped on my window,
the surprise was all over his face?

***

Spiders

It was early in the morning and I was fast asleep in bed,
Laying star-shaped as you do,
when a thud landed by my head.
It woke me up immediately and I fumbled for the light,
And there was a massive spider on the pillow, to the right.
With some rubber gloves on and a pair of shoes –
my God I must've looked a sight,
And if anyone had seen me they would've said,
"that's a dizzy blonde alright!"
I ran to get a book, ironically of *Guns in the Civil War*!
And I thought if I could possibly brave it,
I could throw it from the door.
But I wasn't brave enough
and I was scared it would run away,
So I opted for the fly killer and the whole can I did spray.
All very clever – yeah, but the thing shot under my bed,
I'll never get it I thought
and where it would crawl, I dread.
This was getting quite ridiculous
and I didn't know what to do,
I was crying in shear panic
and it had now gone half past two.
I picked up my phone and rang my Mum who thought
something was seriously wrong,
"It is,"

I said,
"a
spider
dropped,
and
nearly
landed
on
my
head."
"Well do you think my darling," she said,
"at the age of forty-three,
You ought to come back home to Mum
and spend a night with me?!"
I really did consider it
but barricaded the door round the floor,
With lots of pillows and blankets,
and then slept in the bed next door.
Needless to say, I never slept a wink,
and the next morning what did I see –
That damn thing by the window,
almost sniggering back at me.
I'd had enough and it not being dark
and braver than before,
I whacked it with a pillow and it curled up on the floor.
Don't tell me I am cruel, I'm sorry but it has to be said –
For me there's only one way to have a spider –
out of your house, or even dead!

The Pier

I dropped my daughter off at school
At the top of the drive by the gates,
"Now don't forget Mum, stick to the diet,"
She said, "See you at three don't be late."
So with time on my hands, I went into town
And parked right down by the sea,
Unfortunately, though across from my car
The chip shop was open – yippee!
I read my book with one eye on the shop
And smells that were hitting my tum,
It's no good I thought my daughter won't know,
I had to – it had to be done.
So I sat in my car with window right down
And savoured each mouthful with glee,
All I need now is a drink to complete it
And luckily Budgens sold tea.
How handy the tea just as you went in,
Right by the staff room door,
But then I noticed a pack of jam doughnuts,

'Buy six for the price of just four.'
Oh no, I thought do I really need them
As I remembered the words of my daughter,
The coffee was fine yeah I could have that,
But doughnuts – I didn't oughter!
Needless to say I was back in my car
Sipping coffee and leaning on door,
And before you could say Jack Robinson –
I'd eaten not one – but FOUR!
So feeling quite sick and waistband so tight,
I took a stroll down to the pier,
And popped to the toilet and was washing my hands
When the sobbing I couldn't help but hear.
I went back in the toilet and closed the door
Till I knew the coast was clear,
In what seemed like ages the person came out,
It was then that I started to fear.
I thought it was drugs that had caused my concern,
But then I noticed on top of the loo,
The pregnancy test the person had done
Had changed from a pink to a blue.
I sat on the pier in the cubicle seats
And noticed the girl on the end,
Was sobbing her heart out and very distressed,
She looked like she needed a friend.
I sat down beside her and said, "You ok?
I found the test in the loo;
Put two and two together

Then realised immediately the person
this belonged to was you."
I bought her an ice cream to settle her down,
And I thought it would help pave the way,
We discussed at great length what was to be done,
Cos this babe wasn't going away.
We talked it all through for what seemed like hours,
For this young girl it all was a blur,
I gave her my name and my number,
And if all failed, I'd be there for her.
I gave her a hug and said my goodbyes,
She'd a lot to sort out in her mind –
Who knows, it might be that she'll give me a call
And arrive on my doorstep I'll find!
I returned to the school, Ann was standing alone
In the sun by the poplar trees,
Still feeling quite full she hopped in the car
And said, "Can we buy an ice cream please?"
Just what could I say having stuffed myself silly,
If it were your daughter, what would you do?
So she nipped in the shop and returned with a smile
And said, "Here Mum – I got one for you!"

These next few poems were written just after I moved into my house, It's amazing what you can do when you have to but boy did that put me to the test and my patience let me tell you!

My First attempt at Wallpapering!

When I moved into my little house
The walls were very plain,
All in a tone of yellow
And each one looked the same.
So while sitting in my downstairs loo
And wondering what to do,
I thought, "I know I'll wallpaper it
Yep that's what I'm gonna do."
I was in between my jobs
Working away as a maternity nurse,
The hours were long and I got very tired,
But I loved it and so did my purse.
I knew just what I wanted,
Something bold that might be seen
While sitting in the living room
And fit to show the Queen.
I did eventually find it,
Maroon with big flowers,
The pattern looked an easy one,
It shouldn't take me hours.
With lack of tools and no work table,
I pasted on the top
Of the kitchen surface
I slapped it on and was getting very hot.
While stood on the loo I put it up

And pressed it so in line,
And with kitchen knife I cut the edge
Till soon it looked just fine.
I started this at 11 p.m.
It took so long to do,
And before I even realised,
It was almost ten to two.
So I started early
On the very next day.
I was working round the door,
But it stuck to my back,
Fell on my head,
And slithered to the floor.
Another piece was needed,
This wallpapering wasn't my sport,
I measured and pasted and reached for the top,
But the bottom was way too short!
I have to say it's the most stressful thing
I think I have EVER done,
It tops divorce and moving house
I'd make it number one.
In between my work I'd hang another and fix,
And what should have taken just three days
In a total of months
Took SIX!

***

The Chandelier

It's taken me simply ages
To find the perfect one,
My bedroom chandelier I mean –
Not a tall dark hunky man.
I've been scouting the shops for weeks,
And thinking to myself,
There must be something that I like
And there it was on the shelf.

Absolutely perfect
Painted in light cream,
With prinkity glass things that dangled down,
My God it looked a dream.

I got a friend to fit it,
As I really didn't know
A thing about electrics,
Or where the wires should go.
The screws that were provided
Weren't long enough to grip,
The fixture to the ceiling
And it constantly would slip.
It held for several hours,
Until the middle of the night
When a massive crack awoke me,
And gave me quite a fright.
So on the way to school next day
I stopped off at the shop,
And asked the lad for two longer screws,
And watched his jawline drop.
So with patience wearing slightly thin
And standing on a chair,
I tried to screw the new ones in
But they don't fit the hole that's there.
So back to shop I toddle again
This time greeted by three,
Young men standing proudly
Looking back at me.

"The screws you sold me yesterday,"
I said, "are far too thick" –
He said "You come with me my booty,
I'll find you one that'll fit!"
So with my 80p on counter
I looked up at these men,
And said, "I bet you're hoping these don't fit
So I'll have to come back again!"
My lovely chandelier was hanging by a thread,
So with one foot on the chair and the other on the bed,
I pushed the screw up in the hole,
At last it took a grip,
But not for long –
It fell back down,
I was beginning to feel a twit.

Who would think a simple task
Of screwing light to ceiling
Would end up such a nightmare,
For me it wasn't appealing.
I've given up with the screwing bit
And in the tool box I did see,
The mighty hammer, that'll do the trick,
One whack, it's in – yippee.

I thought the job was over,
till I looked across to see,
The little
prinkity
glassy things
That could only be hung by me.
I'd really got a sweat on
And my patience I just can't say,
But give me a roll of wallpaper,
I'd do it any day.

Alton Towers

It was the summer of 2010
that I took the children from work,
To Alton Towers with a member of staff –
Ann thought I must be berserk.

Of all the people on this earth
I am the one who'll hide,
as I have the weakest stomach
for upside-downy rides.

Every ride was ridden
their faces you should have seen,
and I was in charge of videoing
which turned out to be a scream.

Me and technology I'm a nightmare
and it drives me mad,
so you can imagine the video footage –
it was well and truly sad!

Excellent pictures of the sky
and people's legs looked great,
but I laughed and giggled at them all so much
it made my hands just shake.

I was eventually persuaded and Kate said,
"Don't be lame," so I chose a ride called RITA,
the name it sounded tame –

and just to make it worse

I chose the line with no queue,
it was only when
they rammed me in –
I'd chosen front row view!

There are no words to describe it,
I was terrified that's a fact,
and it shot from 0–160
in two and a half seconds flat.

I was catapulted like a rocket –
Kate never made a sound
and I absolutely screamed my head off
the whole 40 seconds round.

My legs they felt like jelly,
I felt as if I'd had wings
"You kept on screaming," said Katie
"and you didn't see a thing."

I had the picture taken
to prove that I had been –
the bravest carer in the world
Alton Towers had ever seen!

***

The Ladybird Infestation

I arrived to do my night shift at work which is near the coast, luckily there's always a breeze there but inland it's as warm as toast.

I grabbed my bag and was quite surprised when stood by the kitchen door as I was attacked by loads of ladybirds, and they were splattered all over the floor.

The walls, floors, just everything seemed to be alive with the little red things, that crawled their way in nooks and crannies, cos these little devils have wings.

I sat in the office for change over and before they'd even said "Mary" those little buggers were stampeding me, I'm telling you it was really quite scary.

I took a walk to the local shop – well what a job that turned out to be – they dive- bombed us and stuck to our hair and the roads were alive like the sea.

I've never seen anything like it before, and where the banks should have been mud, were thousands of dead ladybirds, that was weird and looked at a glance just like blood.

Going to bed was alarming as I opened my bedroom door,
the carpet was a minefield of red, I've never seen this before.

As I lay in my bed aware of the noise of them clicking,
they all seemed too near, and I shot under the covers I
really was scared that one would crawl into my ear.

I don't know how but at some point I did manage to nod
off to sleep, but was suddenly awakened as I kicked off my
covers as one had crawled over my feet.

So with tissue in ears and cocooned in my bed, I sweated
it out with these blighters, and if anything else the amount
that I lost, I must've weighed half a stone lighter.

***

The Job in Worcester and the Sick Baby

I took a job in Worcester
For a lovely family, I could tell,
Where Mum was away on holiday,
So I had baby Annabelle.
At five weeks she was adorable,
Though feeding was a chore
As top up feeds were endless
And she constantly asked for more.
I decided pretty quickly
And as not to make a song
That a stronger milk was needed
To satisfy babe the whole night long.
So down to Tesco I toddled,
Unbeknown to me
It was the largest one for miles
And in the distance I could see.
It simply was amazing
With an escalator as you went in,
And I must have looked astonished
As I made the security chap grin.
So down the isles I trotted.
It's amazing what you see,
The milk is so expensive
Shame it's not buy-one-get-one-free.
So up the escalator I went

To find the stand with clothes,
And turning round the corner
I saw a lady on her toes –
Reaching for the skirt
Which looked size 8 to me.
This lady wouldn't get in that
She was a biggen I could see.
So back to house I dashed
To feed the babe this milk at three,
It seemed to do the trick
She looked more content to me.
The baby had a stinking cold
Which reached its peak in night,
And a sudden coughing noise
Awoke me with a fright.
So down to surgery next morning
I drove her in my car –
"It won't take long to get there,"
Said Sal, "It really isn't far."
We sat down in the surgery
Waiting to be seen,
A man walked in with gun boots on
And a jacket that was dirty and green.
Everyone seemed to know him
Which made him feel quite proud,
And more he talked, the quieter it got
And his voice appeared quite loud.
But what caught his eye was the lady

With the wavy long blonde hair,
He moved along to make more room,
The seat beside him now was spare.
And as if by magic she spotted him
She couldn't help catch his eyes,
And sat right down beside him –
Now there was a surprise!
They talked and chatted cos they knew everyone
The conversation seemed absurd
And poor old Jack whoever he was
Had been kicked out and she was now on her third!
Eventually they called us in
And checked Annabelle thoroughly,
But before I could say hardly anything,
We were heading for A and E.
It all started getting confusing
When the questions they started to come
Till eventually I had to say "Stop,
you do realise I'm not this child's mum?"
By now the doctor had decided
That he wasn't gonna let us both go,
Till I said, "Look, I know she'll be fine –
I'm a Norland Nanny you know?".
Well that did the trick they seemed gobsmacked
And quickly I was soon seen,
And sent on our way with a letter,
You'd think I'd said I was the Queen.
The baby is far more contented,

And each time Mum rings on the line,
And asks, "Hows my baby doing?"
– We all smile and say "Oh she's just fine!"

***

I do many train journeys to and from London, I actually love the train and it gives me that time to collect my thoughts before my next job etc. This next poem was one that just seemed to stick out more than most –

My next poem was written when I was heading to London on a maternity job and it was one of those occasions that I didn't have any paper to write on so I had to go back to the buffet bar where I'd bought my awful coffee and ask them for some napkins to which I wrote my next poem on. I still have the napkin to this day as memories of that trip!

Sitting on the Train

I'm heading back to London with case and bag in hand,
the centre of the hubbub they say of promised land.

I've been and bought a coffee – a must they say you should, but
it tastes just so disgusting, with nine sugars it's still no good.

So I'm sitting in my seat and staring straight ahead
at a gormless spotty youth with a hat rammed on his head.

He's pierced all round his nose and halfway up his ear,
the lady sat beside him cannot help but stare.

The gentleman just opposite is doing his best to see that
his three young children eat their sandwiches that he'd
made himself you could see.

But this little chubby tearaway wasn't content to sit,
instead he stood up with his crispy fingers and poked the
man in front in his head –

Who continued reading his newspaper he was a smart man with a smart job who you could've seen would've loved to have said, "Sit down you little sod".

The young girl sat beside me has completely repainted her face, though clearly has forgot to brush her hair as it looks a real disgrace.

She's finalising lipstick, and sticking nails so neat, with just a spray of perfume her look is now complete.

I wonder who she's meeting that requires doing this on the train, maybe by the way she looks her client has no name!

But my journey's nearly ended so I'll put my pen away —an interesting journey – and so to another day.

***

The Norland Reunion

The date was set for January
At Kit's on Molehill Farm,
Where we could all gather together
For a never-ending yarn.
For me it was a trek
As I set out for six in morning
Having just got over all the snow –
I was faced with a fog warning.
The drive seemed simply endless
Till I eventually found the dot,
And listening to my satnav Cilla
Said "Arriving at the spot."
I walked down to the farmhouse steps
Feeling really quite proud
And when I opened that heavy old door,
The screams were just so loud.
Everyone was hugging and kissing,
And eyes checking out to see,
Who'd aged well, who'd got wrinkles –
Ooh I hope they weren't looking at me.
The catching up was never-ending
And neither was the food,
Kitty gal you did us proud
And kept us in the mood.
Her little boy was gobsmacked

As he sat with toys on floor,
And watched and seemed transfixed with us,
Cos us Norlanders sure can jaw!
Her husband didn't know what hit him
With women everywhere,
And every time I saw him
He grinned from ear to ear.
I looked across at sofa
At the cackling lot to see
The hilarious conversations
It was like the muppets on T.V.
Someone brought their little dog
With jacket and diamond collar,
But Kitty's dog had other ideas
And tried to eat it for her supper.
Nobs said she couldn't come
As the drive scared her to bits,
But having got her ear bent
She turned up at ten to six.
Everybody soon went home
Which left us faithful four,
Gassing and laughing till eventually
We climbed the stairs at four.
But just before we did
Me and Trotts were peckish you see
And rummaged till we found – in the bin,
A charred quiche which looked so good to me.
We scoffed our way through half of it

It really was insane,
We giggled lumped, bumped about,
We'll never be asked back again.
George was sharing a bed with Nobs,
Who was brushing her teeth next door,
But Trots and I had better plans –
We'd hide in the cupboard on the floor.
But having had one too many,
We fell back in the shoes,
All George could hear was laughing
And to her it did amuse.
We were sat amongst the clothes in dark –
Laughing for sure she'd hear,
But I jumped at Trots foot poked at me
And wrapped me round the ear.
It simply was hilarious
If our children could only see –
Two drunk forty-five year olds
Acting as if they were three.
We did eventually retire
And I crawled into my bed,
And i can tell you sat at the table next morning,
I had a thumping head!
What a fabulous time we had
We're gonna do it next time in Bath –
In a hotel for us – well can you imagine
What fun we'll have – what a laugh!

Finding Walnuts

Early in the morning
When most people are in bed,
I water my plants in my jarmies
And make sure that none are dead.
But while I walk around the garden
Which is now looking tidy and neat,
I constantly hear a cracking noise
Underneath my feet.
I can be digging and weeding
Quite happily with not a care in mind,
Yes it's walnuts that I dig up
That a squirrel leaves for me to find.
They bury them all over the garden
To eat at a later date,
And they're hidden pretty cleverly
So not found by another mate.
And while I'm sitting on the patio
Sipping a mug of coffee,
Those little buggers have buried one by me
That has started growing into a tree!

My Fig Tree

I've always wanted a fig tree,
And had one in my garden before
But left it behind when I moved out
Cos I just couldn't take any more.
And when I moved to this house,
Then money was just so tight,
But now it's two years down the line
And the time is simply right.
So purchase I did a fig tree
And planted it on the bank –
So in years when lots of figs appear
It will be myself that I can thank.
But winter was a harsh one
Its leaves dropped and went to sleep
Spring has come, I keep on looking
But no buds have yet to peep.
Every time I drive out
I look and turn my head –
But I think the frost has got it,
And I'm sure that it is dead.
My long-awaited fig tree,
Well, a twig it looks – I fear,
But on close examination
A green thing has appeared.
Several days have passed,

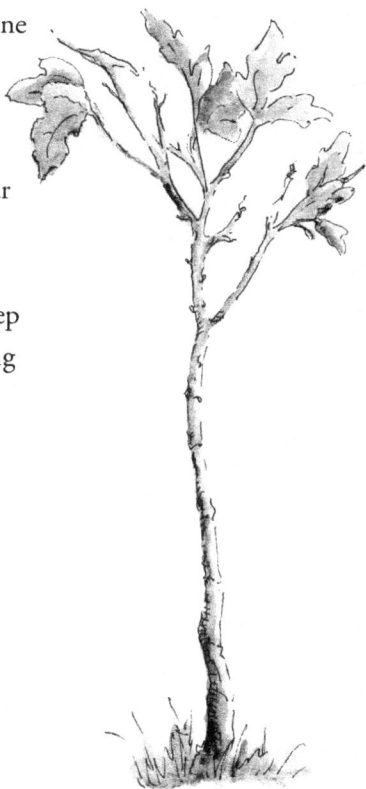

I've watered it to make it thrive –
And much to my amazement
MY FIG TREE IS ALIVE!
It now had four new buds
That have shot out from the side
I WILL have figs eventually
That will ripen in my drive.

***

The 'Take That' Concert at Wembley

I went to see Take That
With some friends at the beginning of June.
They picked me up at six in the morning
Which couldn't have been too soon.
Today I'd be a groupie
And queue for hours... quite sad!
And the more I think and look back on it
It really was just mad.
We eventually arrived at Wembley
And ran to join the queue,
That was slowly beginning to form,
But for now was just a few.
We sat on black bin liners
Which I pulled from in my pockets,
And if it started raining later
They could double up as jackets.
The atmosphere was buzzing
People broke out into song
Singing Abba, and it was funny
That the words were never wrong.
Sharon had taken so much food,
Enough to feed an army,
I had Pimm's and homemade flapjacks,
Which on reflection seemed quite barmy.
The security chaps were funny

And with bribery I have to say,
I forced them to eat my flapjacks
Cos I wasn't gonna throw them away!
The gates were suddenly opened
And we were told to walk not run,
It was like talking to a bunch of school kids
Who wouldn't listen to their mum.
But we made it to the front
And leant against the bars,
"Not long now," said the girl behind –
"Only three more hours"!
The Pet Shop Boys sang first,
The songs which we all knew,
But the youngsters who stood behind us,
You could see hadn't got a clue!
Eventually this was it –
Robbie was the first one on,
Taking the stage alone
With the famous 'Angels' song.
The rest of That soon joined him
And strutted and sang on their stands
Then walked right down to where we stood
And came and shook our hands.
It really was a day to remember,
One I won't forget,
And someone must've been looking down on us
As we didn't even get wet.

My Garden

I simply love my garden
and it's coming on a treat –
I've got a border now
And with shrubs that look quite sweet.
Tony was my gardener
And I've known him many years,
He's witnessed my way of gardening,
which has reduced him sometimes to tears.
Unlike him, I still haven't grasped
What's a weed or what's a plant
but I reckon for me if in doubt –
don't think twice, just pull it out!

***

Growing Veg

Every year I say
"I'm going to grow some veg."
I could grow them in a border
Or dot them round the edge,
But spring crept up quite quickly
So I didn't have that long –
To rummage for containers
Till I found them – oh ding dong!
There was buckets, pots and bins
That lent themselves all well,
But the thing that caught my eye
Was the parrot cage base I could tell.
It's tall and big and round
With the top bit not too deep,
The soil will fit in perfectly
To grow some seeds a treat.
So I sprinkled and placed and stood them,
By the garage door somehow,
And Ann said "Mum we really can say
That we're real Cabbage Patch Kids now!"

The Mystery of the Garden Gnome!

I was on the phone this morning
to my mum who was ill in the night,
When I gazed out of the window
and a green thing caught my sight,
Balanced under the bush,
Had grown just like a seed,
Was nothing more than a garden gnome
with a bucket in each hand indeed.
Just what the heck or who?
Exactly had put him in his place,
Precariously balanced
with a smile upon his face.
I've rang and text all the male acquaintances,
who I think could be to blame,
But the response has come back negative,
with the answers all the same.
And to this day I still don't know,
which one of you is playing the moose,
I sincerely hope though that this little gnome
Doesn't go and **reproduce**!

Epilogue

Time has moved on for me since writing this book...
Not much...
I am now happily married to a wonderful man, who I have
to say has the patience of a saint as he helped me to put the
final stages of this book together which let me tell you was
very tedious for him as I pressed erased and moved things
to all the wrong places, but thankyou darling...
that's why you love me!!!
It took me some finding him,
I might add
But then...
That is another story !!!!!!

Thanks

Writing this book for me came at a time when I was at a low and I didn't even realise what fun writing can be. I can write about anything and anybody in my way, which I know probably isn't politically 'correct' but hey that's me I'm just a Norfolk Bird.

I would like to thank my friend Mark, who helped, guided and pushed me on, giving me concrete advice. Also I would like to thank my cousin Ros who sat for hours and hours writing, sorting and putting it altogether, between caramel squares, coffee and delicious snacks. Then there is my sister who has done the illustrations for me…Thank you so much Libby.

Finally, a big thank you to all of my friends and family who constantly kept saying… do it.

Well I have.